A House With No Windows

MIKE JOHNSON   INGRID BERZINS

Bean Sprout Press

so he went to ask the jade rabbit

who'd been digging holes in the moon

for all eternity (it's easy to see them!)

to ask for advice

you can't ask me, the rabbit said, because

I dig burrows and burrows don't have

windows, silly — deep underground

there is a burrow heaven

and it has no windows

you can't ask me, the woodcutter said

I have no time, I'm too busy to look around

and can only see your light

in the blade of my axe

so the man in the moon went to the goddess

who lives in the mountains of the moon

in a splendid palace of ice

you can't ask me, she said, I've been

banished from the earth forever

because I stole my king's elixir

and so a house without windows

is just like my heart, all closed off

and shut away

this made the man in the moon even sadder

he couldn't shine in the rabbit's burrow

he could only shine on the woodcutter's blade

he couldn't shine in the goddess's heart

he couldn't even shine on the foolish toys

who forgot to put windows in their houses

of bricks and sand and sticky stuff

but there was love in his heart, even for the poor

chipped and broken toys with their eyes rubbed out

and their houses with no windows, no doors even,

so he turned his sad face away,

to the other side, the dark side

where the stars alone could see his tears

and his bright and happy face might always

be looking our way

Bean Sprout Press,
an imprint of Lasavia Publishing Ltd.
Auckland, New Zealand

www.lasaviapublishing.com

© Poems: Mike Johnson, 2020
© Illustrations: Ingrid Berzins, 2020

This book is copyright. Apart from any fair dealing for the purpose of private study, research, criticism or reviews, as permitted under the Copyright Act, no part may be reproduced by any process without the permission of the publishers.

ISBN: 978-0-9951398-6-2

www.ingramcontent.com/pod-product-compliance
Lightning Source LLC
Chambersburg PA
CBHW041442010526
44118CB00003B/156